The Slanted Lens™

Photocomics by JAY P. MORGAN

General Publishing Group, Inc.
Los Angeles

PUBLISHER: W. Quay Hays
EDITORIAL DIRECTOR: Peter Hoffman
ART DIRECTOR: Kurt Wahlner
PRODUCTION DIRECTOR: Trudihope Schlomowitz
COLOR AND PREPRESS MANAGER: Bill Castillo
PRODUCTION ARTIST: Gaston Moraga
PRODUCTION ASSISTANTS: David Chadderdon, Tom Archibeque, Gus Dawson, Russell Lockwood, Regina Troyer, Roy Penn

For information:
General Publishing Group, Inc.
2701 Ocean Park Boulevard
Santa Monica, California 90405

Library of Congress Cataloging-in-Publication Data

Morgan, Jay P.
    The slanted lens / photocomics by Jay P. Morgan.
        p.   cm.
    ISBN 1-57544-034-2
    1. Photography—Humor. 2. American wit and humor, Pictorial.
    I. Title.
TR147.M65   1997
779'.092—dc21   97-34432
                                                                  CIP

Printed in the USA
by RR Donnelley & Sons Company
10 9 8 7 6 5 4 3 2 1

General Publishing Group
Los Angeles

For Julene, my wife,
without whom life wouldn't be so sweet,
and I couldn't accomplish so much.

For Kelly, the driving force behind it all.

Acknowledgments

Special thanks to Philip Collins for introducing us to General Publishing Group; to Quay Hays, Peter Hoffman and the gang at GPG for their faith in this work; to Julene Morgan for her tireless editing, advice, and direction on this book and in my life; to Kelly Keith Morgan for keeping the fire burning under the whole Slanted Lens project; to the staff at Jay P. Morgan Pictures—full time and freelance—for all they do each day; to Elinor Hayden for lightening my work load; to Whoopi Goldberg, Andy Dick, Judge Reinhold, Elvira, Tim Frisbie and all the models and talent for bringing the photographs to life; to each and every crew member for helping to create this work; to Elayne Boosler, Sandra Watkins, Mike Palleschi, David Jouris, Ken and Dennis Agle, Ken Raines, Julene Morgan, Adam Consolo, and Robert Harding for their help on captions; to Jim Boulden of Animal Makers for all his incredible animals; to Nick Nichols who didn't need to help me but did so willingly; to my mother Jylene Morgan for her enthusiasm and support; to my father James Morgan who literally built the Studio; to my in-laws for providing me with so much good material; and thanks in advance to any one demented enough to laugh at this work.

—JAY P. MORGAN

Sheri's cooking came as a post-honeymoon surprise.

We all turn out like our parents eventually.

It's that time of the month again.

In her effort to unclog the bathroom drain, Edna gave Ernie weeks of unexpected regularity.

Milt and Myrna couldn't afford a trip to Hawaii so they bought some snappy outfits instead.

"Get a dog," you said. "It'll be fun," you said.

If Doug thought getting married would have changed any of this he'd have done it years ago

Bill's wife's decision to remodel the house caught him by surprise.

Judy had a well-deserved reputation as a dynamite cook.

Just when the Hardings got rid of their ant problem, a new pest arrived.

In spite of her innocent appearance, Louise always cheated at bingo.

A big sale always brings the heifers in from the country.

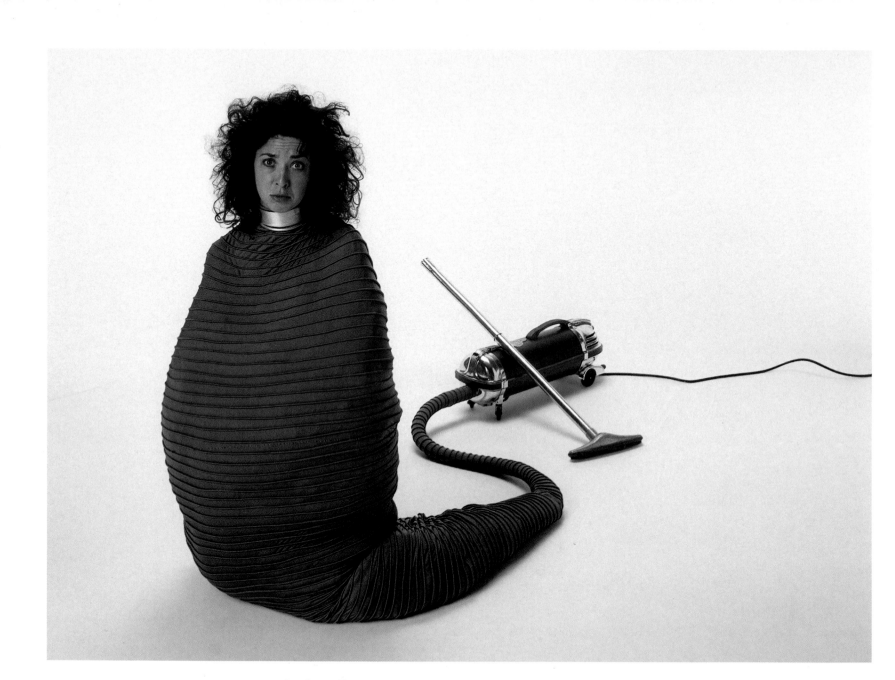

In Carol's case, housework especially sucked.

The first sign of postal worker burnout is overstuffing mail boxes with excessive junk mail.

Just a simple basement band with more amps than brains

The rent was cheap but the neighborhood was hell. . . what's a girl to do?

12:02 and Larry has already broken his resolution not to make a fool of himself in public.

After 50 years of marriage, Lillian tried to spice things up: Tuesdays were rodeo nights.

Rich couldn't remember if he'd picked up his date yet or not.

Whoopi realized that there was nothing like an L.A. morning to get your adrenaline going.

It all started with Kate's need for a small hobby.

This isn't exactly what Joe and Sandra had in mind when they got a watch dog.

Happy Mother's Day!

The kids realized that to get dad to exercise, they had to use the right incentive.

Milt was protesting the annual visit to his mother-in-law's house.

If this was another one of Mr. Pearson's advances, Edna wasn't impressed.

Ted was demonstrating postal tendencies.

Myrna's exposure to the zoo was complete.

Unfortunately for the Morgans, they were the next stop after the baker's house.

Behind every great man there is a disgusted woman.

Jason had just cut his practice time in half.

Darrell had wondered what the extra bolts were for.

Deck the walls with skids from Harleys.

Frank wondered if waiving the rental car insurance was such a good idea.

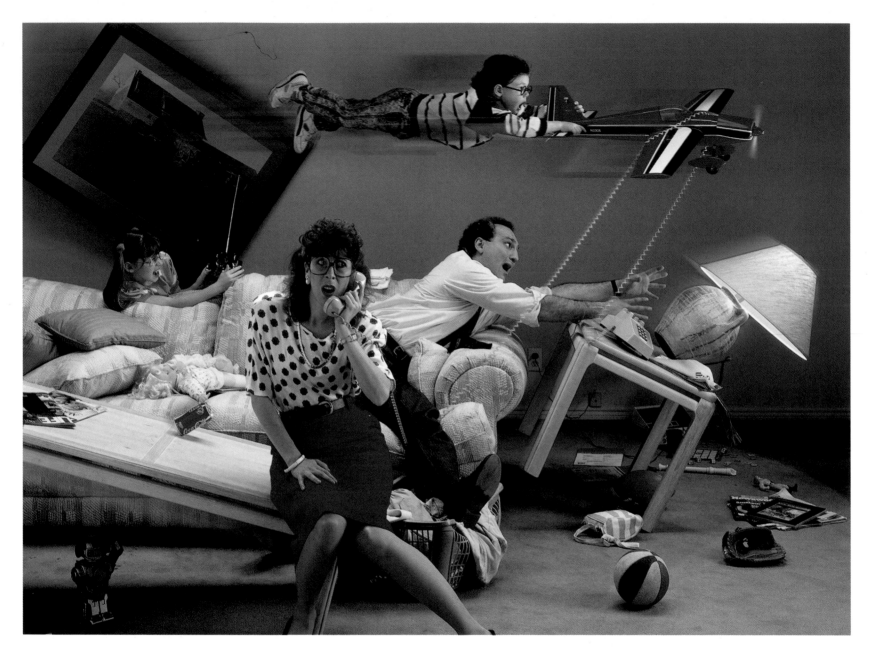

"…No, we've really been disciplining them since the last time you babysat… Great!… we'll pick you up at six"

Kelly's parents never thought they'd miss the day he gave up the trombone.

I'd like a birth control pill please!

Safe Sex!

Jessica's only thought was, "Dad is going to freak when he sees the size of this trout!"

Matt got more spring off his jump than he expected.

It's a wonder that parents survive children.

A simple response to an irritating bird.

The vacation would be remembered as the one when dad couldn't sit on the drive home.

He finally understood why they were always jumping out of their bowl.

Two-legged cockroaches.

Eight chocolate bunnies later Patrick was swinging from the chandelier.

It's not easy being raised by a mother who's a bargain hunter.

"Take your brother for a spin" probably meant on a bike.

"My dad promised me a pool this summer if I got straight A's."

Emily hoped that a giant bird hadn't just passed overhead.

Brad gave new meaning to the term "Tree Hugger."

Yoshi felt naked without his protective eyewear.

Black diamond runs are no place for an engineer with an office chair figure

A woman skiing in a string bikini is a rare sight in January. . . just ask Bill.

This was the last time Bernard waxed his skis with WD-40.

The endangered Red-Turfed Woodpecker outlived most of the ice climbers in the area.

Sean finally caught a killer wave.

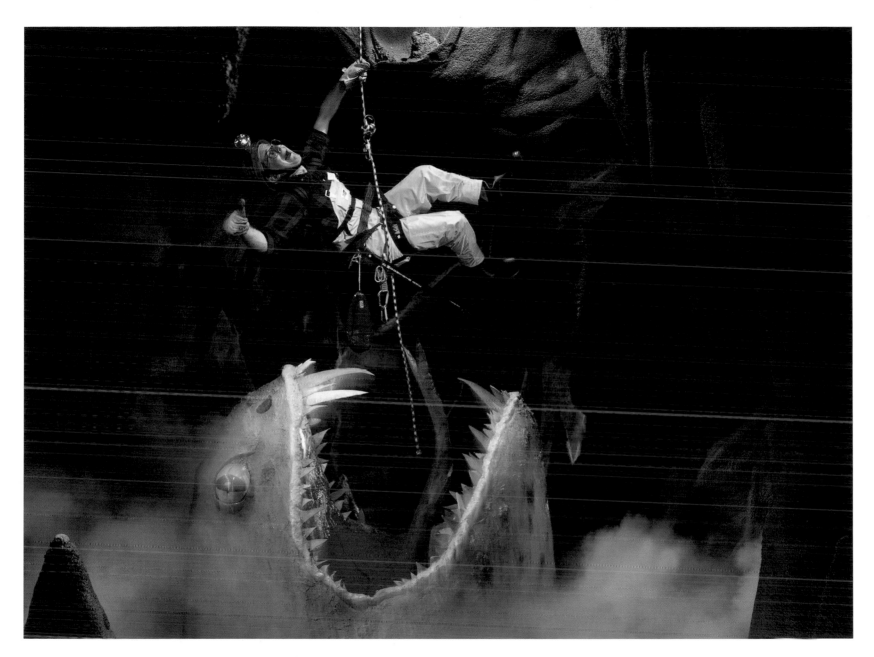

Official Government Statement: Underground nuclear testing has no effect on the ecological systems in this area.

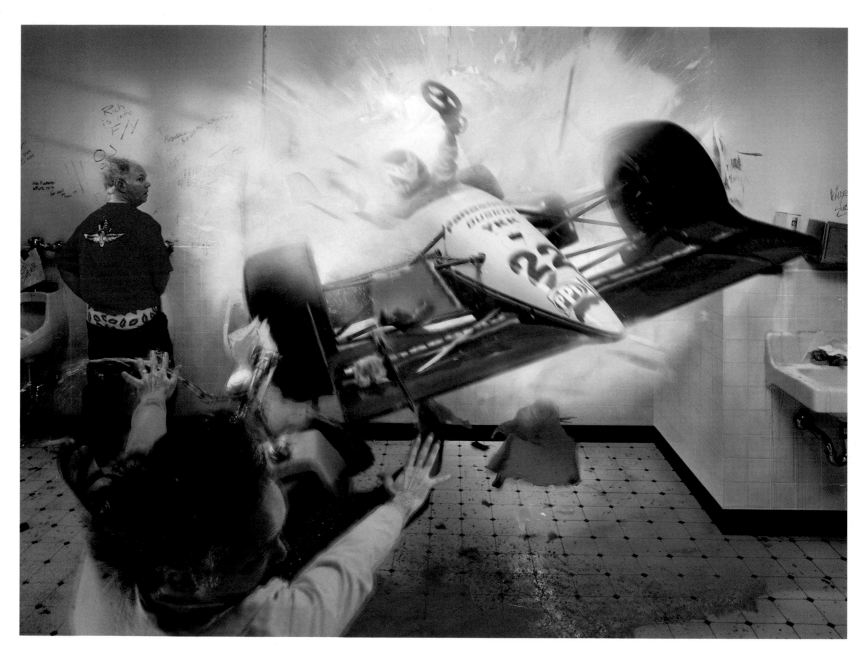

Suddenly the smell of gas was overwhelming.

Jim left the stadium long before his ride was over.

When the buzzards arrived, "Putts" McNabb lost all hope of making par.

"Putts" follows his worst drive with a hole in roof.

When Tim finally dropped out of sight, others felt comfortable playing through.

Extreme Golf!

Like any good marriage, Nick shouted instructions, and Myrna didn't listen.

Troop 106's motto: "Be prepared to run like crazy if Scoutmaster Bob gets a hold of the ball."

Jane knew she should have let her nail polish dry longer.

Boyd needed to work on his release.

Bowlers can be very touchy about their scores.

No one seemed to care that she couldn't play pool.

George regretted giving the cruise recreation director such a teeny tip.

Ernie's Whale Watching. No one gets you closer!

Yet another father/son outing that would lead to years of expensive therapy.

Nick's 2:00 am start didn't serve him as well as he had hoped.

Suddenly, Santa realized why Ned had asked for a case of barbeque sauce.

Leroy woke in a cold sweat wrapped in his wife's arms.

Nessie made a fine trophy and tasted just like chicken.

Mr. Wright was unaware that as the clubhouse went up, his garage was coming down.

As an executive, Judge's life had been torked up a little too tight.

Upon review of the divorce settlement, Ed fired his lawyer.

DR. BARRY N.E.MA
PROCTOLOGIST

Norman realized this doctor was a bum referral.

After three hours of answering phones the new girl took her break and never came back.

The recall notice for Harlan's office chair was held up in the mail room.

It was obvious to Mark that the company was in serious need of downsizing.

Where beauty school dropouts go to make a living.

Hey diddle, diddle, the cat and the fiddle, the cow didn't quite make it over the moon. . . .

No one was as surprised as Chuck to find life on Mars.

The plutonium-powered flushing device backfired.

Ken was an accountant who volunteered on the weekends.

Darrell had hoped that this job would last longer than a week.

Elmer was just saying, "Nothing interesting ever happens in this podunk town."

Santa's gift to the L.A.P.D. each year was a few anonymous tips about people from his naughty list.

Wendal finally worked his way up to a high-impact job.

Once spooked, nothing stops a stampeding Pogo Heifer like a prairie dog hole.

And we heard him exclaim #@*#! as his sleigh drove out of sight.

Behind The Slanted Lens

I've always felt like a cartoonist trapped in an advertising photographer's body. I don't draw (that's an understatement) and I've spent many years creating photography for advertising, neither of which would lead you to think that I should be a cartoonist. However, I've always had the desire to create something that will entertain people. So I used the tools that I possess and came up with a photographic comic.

Unlike that of a traditional cartoonist, my studio does things in a very big way. We have to search for special props, cast for particular talent, bring in animals and their trainers, hire photography assistants, invent special rigging and build sets that defy gravity, allowing us to execute each image in one shot right in front of the camera's lens. This calls for long hours of exhausting work. It's certainly more fun to look back at the process than it is to be in the middle of it.

There is always some difficult challenge to overcome. You do all the preparation you can and it's still managed mayhem when you get to the shoot. There was the time Santa showed up on crutches without his artificial leg. "Bill, where's your leg," we asked. "Well it was hurting so I didn't bring it." "Bill, most people think that Santa has two legs. I know its a politically incorrect assumption, but no leg is a problem." We sent the assistants to carve a leg for Santa so he could be suspended on the TV antenna. This is how it all goes. We could do it on the computer but the excitement of the process would be lost and I think the look would be lost as well. It's not to say that we don't use the computer, because on occasion we do. However, we generally get it as far as we can before we let the computer help out.

There is nothing as satisfying as being in the trenches struggling to get the shot and finally pulling that final Polaroid and realizing that its all going to work. Then you panic once again because you want to shoot it before you lose that fleeting moment when all is in place.

Yes, the defining fear in my life—to capture the moment before it escapes.

— JAY P. MORGAN